S0-BZQ-405

First published in Great Britain in 1996 by
Brockhampton Press,
20 Bloomsbury Street,
London WC1B 3QA.
A member of the Hodder Headline Group.

This series of little gift books was made by Frances Banfield, Andrea P. A. Belloli, Polly Boyd, Kate Brown, Stefano Carantini, Laurel Clark, Penny Clarke, Clive Collins, Jack Cooper, Melanie Cumming, Nick Diggory, John Dunne, Deborah Gill, David Goodman, Paul Gregory, Douglas Hall, Lucinda Hawksley, Maureen Hill, Dicky Howett, Dennis Hovell, Nick Hutchison, Douglas Ingram, Helen Johnson, C.M. Lee, Simon London, Irene Lyford, John Maxwell, Patrick McCreeth, Morse Modaberi, Tara Neill, Sonya Newland, Anne Newman, Grant Oliver, Ian Powling, Terry Price, Michelle Rogers, Mike Seabrook, Nigel Soper, Karen Sullivan and Nick Wells.

Compilation and selection copyright © 1996 Brockhampton Press.

All rights reserved. No part of this publication may be reproduced, stored in a retrieval system, or transmitted in any form or by any means, without the prior written permission of the copyright holder.

ISBN 1 86019 4540

A copy of the CIP data is available from the
British Library upon request.

Produced for Brockhampton Press by Flame Tree Publishing,
a part of The Foundry Creative Media Company Limited,
The Long House, Antrobus Road, Chiswick W4 5HY.

Printed and bound in Italy by L.E.G.O. Spa.

The Funny Book of
AFTER DINNER
STORIES

Selected by
Karen Sullivan

Cartoons by
DICKY HOWETT

BROCKHAMPTON PRESS

"By popular request again this year, we'll now have 30 minutes of total silence."

6

A narrow mind and a wide mouth
usually go together.

Anonymous

When in doubt, mumble: when in trouble,
delegate: when in charge, ponder.

James H. Boren

The difference between an amateur and a
professional is that one gets paid and the
other doesn't. For example, as Malcolm
Allison remarks, the Ark was built by
amateurs, the Titanic by professionals.

Mike Seabrook

Blessed is he, who having nothing to say, refrains
from giving wordy evidence of that fact.

Anonymous

Abasement: a decent and customary mental attitude in the presence of wealth and power. Peculiarly appropriate in an employee when addressing an employer.

Ambrose Bierce, **The Devil's Dictionary**

In the earlier years of the twentieth century, the Rev. Dean Inge (pronounced 'Ing') was Dean of St Paul's Cathedral, but also a prominent figure in public life, a member of the great and the good, a man whose opinions were heeded on all manner of issues; he also wrote a long article regularly for the Evening Standard. Introducing him one evening as the guest speaker at some function, A. P. Herbert said that it was his pleasure to introduce 'not merely a pillar of the Church, but also a couple of columns of the Evening Standard as well.'

Mike Seabrook

"I reckon Batman's over the limit!"

"My husband's a rather unusual after-dinner speaker."

My grandmother is over eighty and still doesn't need glasses. Drinks right out of the bottle.

Henny Youngman

Reminds me of my safari in Africa. Somebody forgot the corkscrew and for several days we had to live on nothing but food and water.

W. C. Fields

I do not object to people looking at their watches when I am speaking. But I strongly object when they start shaking them to make certain they are still going.

Lord Birkett

A few years ago, the chairman of the board of a well-known private school was invited to talk to the student body.

'Well, all right,' said the chairman. 'What subject would you like me to talk about?'

The headmaster replied, 'It would be very helpful if you'd give them a talk about sex.'

After a little hesitation, the chairman accepted. But when he got home, he didn't quite dare tell his wife the subject he was given, so he told a white lie. 'I was asked to talk on sailing.' His wife seemed puzzled but the conversation moved on to other things.

A few days later, a student parent remarked to the chairman's wife, 'Your husband gave a wonderful talk to the student body.'

'I'm amazed,' said the wife. 'He's only done it three times. The first time he got sick to his stomach. The second time his hat blew off. And the third time his foot got caught in the sheet.'

*Eric W. Johnson, **A Treasury of Humour***

"Cheer up! You'll get to like after-dinner speaking."

The advantage of doing one's praising for
oneself is that one can lay it on so thick
and exactly in the right places.

Samuel Butler, **The Way of all Flesh**

Taking the air while they waited for the
bars to open, Michael and Patrick were strolling
across the Ha'penny Bridge in Dublin.
'D'ye know, Moikel,' said Patrick, 'Oi was walking
across dis very bridge at the very moment when dat
President Kennedy was assassinated in Dallas.'
'Jesus, Paddy,' exclaimed Michael,
''twas a narrow escape ye had!'

Mike Seabrook

An after-dinner speech should be like a
girl's dress: long enough to cover the subject
and short enough to be interesting.

Anonymous

"Our speaker tonight is Mr Robert Waran, who used to be BBC Television's Head of Special Effects."

Like a camel I can go without a drink for seven days — and have on several horrible occasions.

Herb Caen

Money is trash, and he that will spend it,
Let him drink merrily, Fortune will send it.

Thomas Dekker

Toast
May all the mistakes in our futures be infinitesimal compared to those in our pasts.

Eileen Mason

Only Irish coffee provides in a single glass all four essential food groups: alcohol, caffeine, sugar and fat.

Alex Levine

"*Must have been that after-dinner
speech you gave about religion...*"

The much-loved and lamented Tommy Cooper once took a long ride in a London taxi. At the end of the journey the driver told him the fare, which he counted out carefully to the last ten pence, and handed to the driver. As he turned away he halted as if struck by an afterthought, turned back to the driver, still waiting expectantly for his tip, and pressed something into his hand, murmuring, 'There's a drink for you.' This time he did walk off. The cabbie watched him go, then opened his hand to see how much the tip came to — and he found a single tea-bag.

Mike Seabrook

Speeches are like steer horns: a point here, a point there, and a lot of bull in between.

Sometimes too much to drink is barely enough.

Mark Twain

"No wonder the punch tastes funny
- that's the goldfish water!"

"*The vicar's always a laugh at parties…*"

Toast

I've drunk to your health in company,
I've drunk to your health alone;
I've drunk to your health so many times,
I've damn near ruined my own.

Anonymous

The Irish republican leader, Eamon De Valera, was speaking in his customary firebrand manner from a soapbox in Dublin when Black and Tan troopers descended on him and whizzed him off to trial and, eventually, nine years' imprisonment by the British for sedition. Eventually the Irish home rule cause was successful, the Irish Free State was founded, and De Valera was released from prison. He went straight back to the place where he had been arrested, found a soapbox, mounted it, and began, 'As I was saying when I was so rudely interrupted . . .'

Mike Seabrook

To spend the time luxuriously
Becomes not men of worth.
Samuel Daniel, **Ulysses and the Siren**

Desperately accustomed as
I am to public speaking . . .
Noel Coward, **speech at Oxford**

There's a hell of a distance between
wise-cracking and wit. Wit has truth in it, wise-
cracking is simply callisthenics with words.
Dorothy Parker, **Paris Review**

Spontaneous speeches are seldom
worth the paper they are written on.
Leslie Henson, **The Observer**

*"No, I haven't suddenly shrunk –
you're standing on my husband!"*

When audiences come to see us authors
lecture, it is largely in the hope that we'll
be funnier to look at than to read.

Sinclair Lewis

Adam and Eve were busy assigning names to
the other creatures they had found in the
Garden of Eden. After a long stint in silence,
Adam slapped one beast on the backside and
said, 'Let's call this one the hippopotamus.'
'Oh?' said Eve, showing the curiosity that she
was to develop into such fine art with such
memorable consequences a little later. 'Why?'
'Well,' said Adam. 'We've been at it for over
two hours, and this one looks more like a
hippopotamus than anything so far.'

Mike Seabrook

"I name this...Oops, silly me – it's the wrong ceremony, isn't it...?

I like the way you always manage to state
the obvious with a sense of real discovery.

Gore Vidal, **The Best Man**

If you want real oratory, the preliminary noggin is
essential. Unless pie-eyed, you cannot hope to grip.

P. G. Wodehouse, **Right Ho, Jeeves**

I am the most spontaneous speaker in the
world because every word, every gesture and
every retort has been carefully rehearsed.

George Bernard Shaw

Oscar Wilde was once asked to nominate his
choice for the hundred best books in all literature.
'I fear it would be impossible,' he replied,
declining, 'since I have written only five.'

Mike Seabrook

The actor Trevor Howard was starring in a film about the Cromwellian period. One night they were due to shoot a night scene on location. He decided it would make more sense for him to change into his Cavalier costume at home and go direct to the location site, rather than endure the discomforts of a draughty caravan in a muddy field at midnight. Accordingly he dressed himself carefully in plumed helmet, buckler, greaves, sword and everything else, got on his motor bike and headed off into the country outside Denham. A little while after he entered open countryside he began to have an eerie feeling that he was being followed. This was confirmed a little later when a police car slipped past and waved him to a halt. A fat, lumbering Sergeant, who had clearly seen everything before, hauled himself out of the driving seat and came slowly back to Howard, waiting a little anxiously astride his machine. As he drew level with Howard, the Sergeant handed him a breathalyzer kit, and said, 'Excuse me, Sir, but would you mind holding this while I blow into it?'

Mike Seabrook

"My husband gets a bit jealous."

It usually takes me more than three weeks
to prepare a good impromptu speech.

Mark Twain

Beware of long speeches and long beards.

George Santayana

If, with the literate, I am
Impelled to try an epigram,
I never seek to take the credit;
We all assume that Oscar said it.

Dorothy Parker, **Not So Deep as a Well**

Too poor for a bribe, and too proud to importune,
He had not the method of making a fortune.

Thomas Gray, **On His Own Character**

"An 'After-Dinner Speaker' eh? Well my advice is stick to the speaking and lay off the dinners!"

31

"*Professor Gilbert will now give us a fascinating talk about his time among the spear-carrying tribes of the Amazon delta...*"

Who doth ambition shun,
And loves to live i' the sun
Seeking the food he eats,
And pleased with what he gets.
*William Shakespeare, **As You Like It***

It is always the best policy to speak the truth,
unless of course you are an exceptionally good liar.
*Jerome K. Jerome, **The Idler***

Conscience is the inner voice that warns
us that someone may be looking.
H. L. Mencken

By the time a man is wise enough to
watch his step he's too old to go anywhere.
Earl Wilson

'I'm going to give you an ultimatum, George,'
said the long-suffering wife, placing her
husband's lunch in front of him after his return
from his regular session at the local pub.
'Oh, yes?' he said without great interest as he
started to eat. 'What's that, then?'
'You're going to have to make a straight
choice,' she said, striving to remain calm in
the face of his studied indifference.
He continued to chew for some time. Just
as she thought he was not going to reply
at all he said, 'What choice is that?'
'You're going to have to choose between me and The
Plasterer's Arms,' she said in a grinding voice.
Once again there was a long interval in which he sat
calmly eating. At last he dabbed his lips with his
napkin and spoke. 'Mmm,' he said. 'I'll have to go
down The Plasterer's and think about that.'

Mike Seabrook

A man should marry someone like himself;
A man should pick an equal for a mate.

Geoffrey Chaucer, **The Miller's Tale**

*"Guess what?
I'm an after-dinner squeaker."*

"You would have thought that even a dalek would
have avoided 'knock-knock-who's-there' jokes..."

I never knew any man in my life who could not bear another's misfortunes perfectly like a Christian.

Alexander Pope, **Thoughts on Various Subjects**

Man is the only animal that blushes. Or needs to.

Mark Twain, **Following the Equator**

A puzzled monkey sat in the British Museum reading room. 'After reading the book of Genesis and the works of Sigmund Freud,' he said, 'I am at something of a loss to know whether I am my brother's keeper or my keeper's brother.'

Mike Seabrook

I always pass on good advice. It is the only thing to do with it. It is never any use to oneself.

Oscar Wilde, **An Ideal Husband**

"Gregory – stop playing
with your olive!"

Let us have wine and women, mirth and laughter,
Sermons and soda-water the day after.

Lord Byron

The youth gets together materials for a bridge
to the moon, and at length the middle-aged
man decides to make a woodshed with them.

Henry David Thoreau

Grey hair is great. Ask anyone who's bald.

Lee Trevino

There are two reasons for drinking: one is,
when you are thirsty, to cure it; the other,
when you are not thirsty, to prevent it. . . .
Prevention is better than cure.

Thomas Love Peacock, **Melincourt**

"I promise I won't make any embarrassing remarks about the bride and groom..."

"*Our guest speaker tonight will tell us of the pitfalls of being a driving instructor...*"

The great Hollywood actor John Barrymore used to tell of his experience in the catastrophic San Francisco earthquake of 1906. One minute, he said, he was sleeping peacefully in his hotel room; the next, he was woken by a violent upheaval, in which the bed was upended, and he was hurled to the floor. As he lay on the floor wondering what had hit him, soldiers burst into the room, made sure that he was alive and in one piece, then peremptorily thrust a shovel into his hands and ordered him to go down the street and help in digging out survivors and bodies. Years later his relative and fellow actor, Ethel Barrymore, was asked if this account was true. 'I can't verify it from personal knowledge,' she said, 'but I can tell you for sure it is true.' 'How do you mean?' asked the interviewer. 'Well,' she said, 'I know it's true, because it was always said in our family that it would take an earthquake to get John out of bed, and the army to put him to work.'

Mike Seabrook

Philosophy is nothing but discretion.

John Seldon, **Table Talk**

One evening President Woodrow Wilson took his fiancée, Edith Galt, to the theatre. One reporter noticed that rather than watching the play, 'the President spent most of his time entertaining Mrs Galt.' Alas! The paper's compositors misspelt the crucial word, so that the final words appeared in print as 'entering Mrs Galt.'

Mike Seabrook

The optimist fell ten storeys.
At each window bar
He shouted to his friends:
'All right so far.'

Anonymous

"Are there any after-life, after-dinner speakers there?"

Two doctors were chatting in an exclusive
Swiss clinic. 'What's the matter with you?'
asked one. 'You seem very depressed.'
'Oh, God,' muttered the other lugubriously.
'I made a catastrophic diagnosis the other day.
The worst diagnosis of my life; and I haven't
stopped thinking about it since.'
'We all make mistakes,' said his colleague
sympathetically. 'It will help to talk about it.
Why not get it off your chest?'
'Well,' said the other, 'I had a man come in
complaining of acute stomach and chest pains.
I examined him, diagnosed indigestion, charged him
eight hundred francs and prescribed a mild antacid.'
'Well, what's the matter with that?' asked the other.
'Didn't it cure him?'
'Oh, yes, it cured him all right. He was as right
as ninepence in twenty-four hours.'
'So what's the problem?' asked the other, mystified.
'Well, the next day I found out he could have
afforded a heart transplant.'

Mike Seabrook

Toast

Champagne for your real friends.
Real pain for your sham friends.

Mike Seabrook
Believed to have been coined by Francis Bacon.

Marriage is nothing but a civil contract.

John Selden, **Table Talk**

A woman wants the self-same sovereignty
Over her husband as over her lover,
And master him; he must not be above her.

Geoffrey Chaucer, **The Wife of Bath's Tale**

After dinner rest a while,
after supper walk a mile.

Proverb

"That was a long speech! The last I heard the bride and groom have had two kids and since divorced..."

An elderly spinster was seated in a railway compartment opposite a scruffy young man who, as soon as the train got under way, fell asleep. Unknown to him, his fly was gaping open, and the old lady could not help observing that in time the motion of the train had a somewhat unfortunate effect.

After watching in horrified fascination for a while she tore her gaze away, reached tentatively across and tapped him on the knee. 'Excuse me, young man,' she said nervously, 'but your . . . er . . . your thing is sticking out.'

He woke up briefly, glanced down at the offending portion of his anatomy, and said, 'You flatter yourself, Madam. It's hanging out,' before immediately going back to sleep.

Mike Seabrook

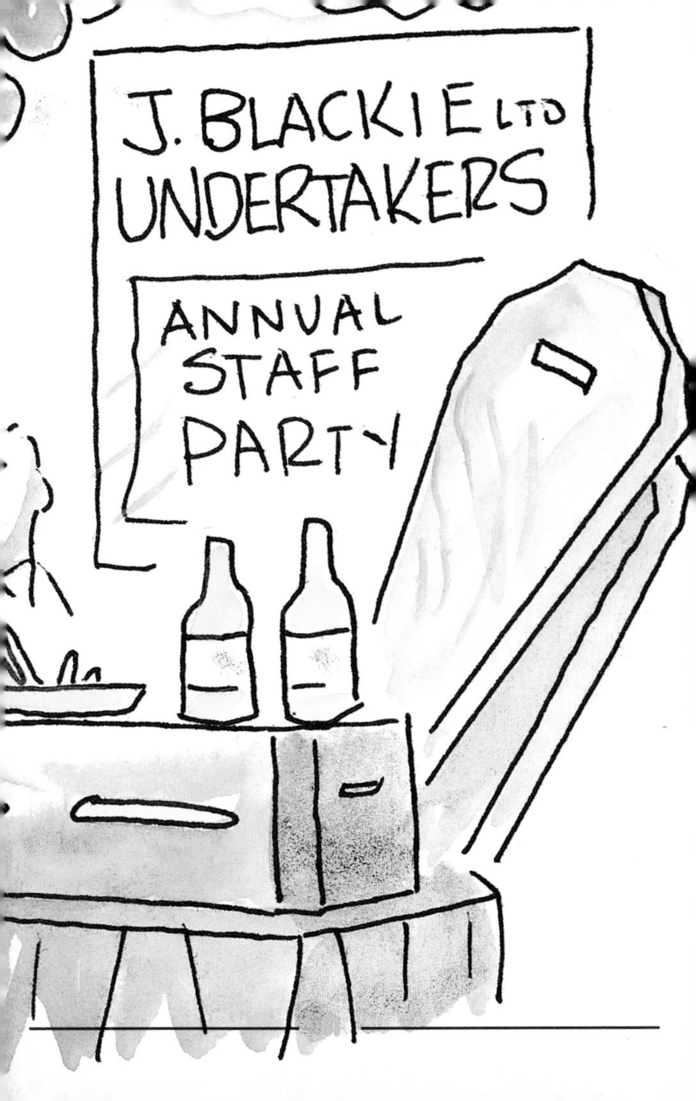
J. BLACKIE LTD
UNDERTAKERS
ANNUAL
STAFF
PARTY

Two motorway patrol policemen, bored and weary as they approached the end of their night shift, were delighted when they spotted a man relieving himself behind the inadequate cover of a bridge stanchion. 'He'll've had one too many, for sure,' said the first officer. 'We'll be spending the rest of the tour in the warm.'

'And I'll get to drive a Roller,' agreed his partner happily as they spotted the Rolls Royce parked on the shoulder thirty yards ahead.

They drew up beside the young man, and the first officer waited while he finished off and adjusted his trousers. Then he went up to him and demanded that he take a breathalyzer test.

The man refused indignantly.

'I haven't been drinking, officer,' he protested. 'Well, only one glass of wine, anyway.' The officer smiled happily, recognizing the signs. The young man still refused indignantly to take the test, however, swearing that he had not had anything like too much to drink, and was duly arrested for refusal.

The arresting officer sped off with him in the police car, en route for the nearest police station, thirty miles distant. His colleague, meanwhile, was left to walk up to the Rolls Royce. When he reached it, happily looking forward to his first drive of such a magnificent car, he was surprised to be greeted by a uniformed and peak-capped chauffeur sitting in the driving seat reading the paper. Suddenly, assailed by horrible doubts, the officer established that the young man they had arrested was the chauffeur's employer.

'Er . . . I wonder . . . would you mind giving me a lift to . . .' the officer said hesitantly, naming the police station to which the chauffeur's master had so unwillingly departed.

'As a matter of fact,' said the chauffeur, who had seen everything that had taken place in his rear-view mirror, 'I'd mind that very much indeed.' With which he started the engine, pulled out into the light traffic, and disappeared into the distance.

Mike Seabrook

Rather than be wise
Churning out words,
Better drink your sake
And weep drunken tears.
Otomo Tabito, **In Praise of Sake**

'Tis not the drinking that is
to be blamed, but the excess.
John Seldon, **Table Talk**

Wine is a charm; it heats the blood too,
Cowards it will arm, if the wine be good too;
Quickens the wit, and makes the back able.
Thomas Dekker, **The Sun's Darling**

"Look on the bright side - at least I enjoyed your after-dinner speech!"

"Cloth-ears! I said can you play 'In The Mood'!"

A travelling salesman was about to register at a hotel when he paused, his attention caught by a very attractive woman who was very obviously giving him a message of 'come hither' from the far side of the lobby. He went over to her and, after a few words together, the two of them strolled back to the desk, where they registered as man and wife. After a blissful night the salesman, fatigued but happy, descended to the desk and asked for his bill. He was then outraged to be given an enormous bill for over a thousand pounds.

'This is quite impossible,' he protested, 'I've only been here one night.'

'Quite so, Sir,' said the manager soothingly. 'But your wife, of course, has been here a month.'

Mike Seabrook

"Just keep talking –
I'm taking notes for my
next after-dinner speech."

"Whose bright idea was it to invite an escapologist along to talk to them?"

Acknowledgements:

The Publishers wish to thank everyone who gave permission to reproduce the quotes in this book. Every effort has been made to contact the copyright holders, but in the event that an oversight has occurred, the publishers would be delighted to rectify any omissions in future editions of this book. Quotations attributed to Mike Seabrook were supplied by Mr Seabrook and printed with his permission; Dorothy Parker quotes from *The Best of Dorothy Parker*, first published by Methuen in 1952, reprinted by Gerald Duckworth & Co., © Dorothy Parker, 1956, 1957, 1958, 1959, renewed; *A Treasury of Humor*, by Eric W. Johnson, published by Ivy Book, Ballantine Books © Eric W. Johnson, 1989; P. G. Wodehouse extracts © P. G. Wodehouse, reprinted courtesy of Herbert Jenkins and Penguin Books; George Bernard Shaw, reprinted courtesy of the Society of Authors on behalf of the Estate of George Bernard Shaw.